People of the Bible

The Bible through stories and pictures

Joseph
and the King

Copyright © in this format Belitha Press Ltd, 1983

Illustrations copyright © Chris Molan 1984

Art Director: Treld Bicknell

First published in the United States of America 1984
by Raintree Publishers, Inc.
205 West Highland Avenue, Milwaukee, Wisconsin 53203
in association with Belitha Press Ltd, London.

Conceived, designed and produced by Belitha Press Ltd,
40 Belitha Villas, London N1 1PD

Moody Press Edition 1984

ISBN 0-8024-0400-6

All rights reserved. No part of this book may be reproduced or utilized in any form or by any means, electronic or mechanical, including photocopying, recording, or by any information storage and retrieval system, without permission in writing from the Publisher.

Printed in Hong Kong by South China Printing Co.

Moody Press, a ministry of the Moody Bible Institute, is designed for education, evangelization, and edification. If we may assist you in knowing more about Christ and the Christian life, please write us without obligation: Moody Press, c/o MLM, Chicago, Illinois 60610

Joseph and the King

Retold by Ella K. Lindvall
Pictures by Chris Molan

MOODY PRESS
CHICAGO

Joseph was sad. He was far away from his home and his father.

Joseph's brothers had sold him to some traveling traders. They took him on a long dusty journey to the land of Egypt. There Joseph was sold again—this time to a man named Potiphar, who worked for Pharaoh, the king.

Did God know where Joseph was?

Yes, He did know, and He was getting Joseph ready for a very special job.

Joseph was clever, and everything he was given to do went well. When Potiphar saw that, he made Joseph the overseer in his house. That meant Joseph looked after everything Potiphar had. Potiphar trusted Joseph with all his possessions.

Joseph was a very nice young man. Potiphar's wife saw him and liked him.

But Joseph said, "My master, your husband, has trusted me with everything he has. But you are his wife. It would be very wicked of me to love you."

But Potiphar's wife liked Joseph anyway. She waited until one day she and Joseph were alone in the house. When she took hold of his coat, Joseph ran away so fast that he left the coat in her hand.

Potiphar's wife was very, very angry. She said to Potiphar, "Your Hebrew servant has insulted me."

Of course that was a lie, but now Potiphar became angry. He sent Joseph to the prison where the king's prisoners were kept.

But God knew where Joseph was, and God was getting Joseph ready for a very special job. The jailer soon saw he could trust him. He let Joseph look after the other prisoners.

Not long after that, Pharaoh, the king, became angry with his chief butler and with his chief baker. He sent them both to prison, and there Joseph looked after them.

One night each of them dreamed a dream. The next morning they were both sad.

Joseph asked them, "Why are you so sad?" Then they told him their dreams.

The butler said, "I dreamed I saw a vine with three branches on it. Then I saw buds and blossoms and ripe grapes. I took the grapes and pressed them into Pharaoh's cup. Then I put the cup into Pharaoh's hand."

God made Joseph know what the dream meant. Joseph said, "The three branches are three days. Three days from now Pharaoh will take you back into his palace, and you will hand him his cup of wine just as you used to. When this happens, remember that I'm here in prison. Please try to get me out, for I have done nothing wrong."

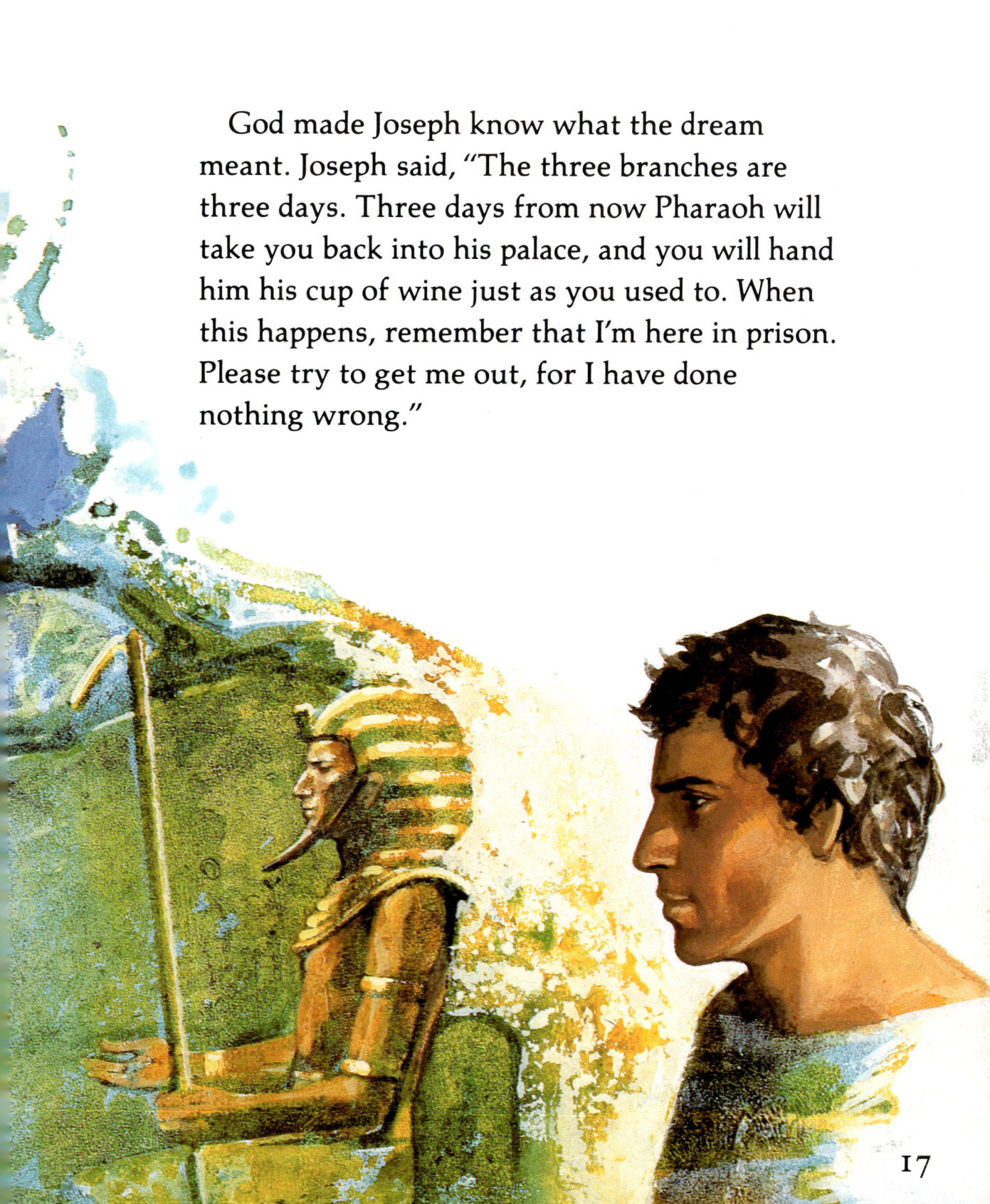

Next the baker told Joseph his dream. "I had three white baskets on my head. In the top one were all kinds of baked food for Pharaoh, but the birds came and ate them all up."

God made Joseph know what this dream meant too. Joseph said, "The three baskets are three days. In three days, Pharaoh will hang you."

What Joseph said about the dreams came true. On the third day, the king hanged the chief baker. He also sent for the chief butler to come back to the palace and take up his old job again. Once the butler was there, he forgot all about Joseph.

But God did not forget him. God was getting Joseph ready for a very special job.

Two long years went by, and Joseph was still in prison. Then one day Pharaoh himself dreamed a dream. He was standing by a river, and he saw seven fat, healthy cattle come out of the river and feed in the meadow. Then he saw seven thin cattle come out of the river and they ate up the fat cattle.

The king woke up. What could such a strange dream mean?

When Pharaoh went back to sleep, he dreamed again. This time he saw seven good ears of grain on one stalk. Then seven thin, bad ears of grain that had been spoiled by the east wind came along and ate the fat ears.

The next morning Pharaoh was troubled. He sent for his wise men. "What do those strange dreams mean?" he asked. But no one could tell him.

Then, at last, the butler remembered. "When the chief baker and I were in prison," he began, "we both had dreams. A man named Joseph told us what our dreams meant."

"Bring Joseph here!" the king ordered.

Down in the prison, Joseph quickly shaved and changed clothes. Then he went to see the king.

When Joseph heard the dreams, he said, "God has shown you what He is going to do."

Joseph said, "The seven cattle and the seven ears of grain mean seven years. For the next seven years there will be plenty of grain in Egypt. But after that there will be seven years when food will not grow. People will be very hungry.

"Let Pharaoh look for a very wise man to rule the land," Joseph then said. "Have the man make sure that part of all the grain is stored away in the seven good years. Then there will be enough food for the people to eat when the seven bad years come."

Pharaoh said, "You have spoken well and wisely. *You* shall rule Egypt under me."

Pharaoh then took a ring off his own finger and put it on Joseph's finger.

He gave Joseph a golden chain for his neck. He gave him fine clothes to wear. And for the next seven years Joseph went around the

country, gathering up more sacks of grain than he could count. Now when the bad years came, the people would have food to eat.

God had made Joseph ready for a very special job indeed.